This book is presented as a Gift to:

_____

From:

_____

Date:

_____

Live Life to the Fullest on Your Terms

Unlock the Treasures of Your Thoughts

Thank you for Dreaming BIG!
If you're looking for the perfect
motivation, inspiration & empowerment,
you're at the right destination.

Think Big, Achieve BIGGER

The Little Black Book of Success
in the Workplace & Life

The Road to Success Begins with a BIG Idea
The Little Black Book with BIG Ideas

J. B. Love

Parts of this book came from J. B. Love's *Anticipation, 10 Keys to Turning Your Dreams into Reality, Love, Life & Courage (Poetry for the Soul)* and *How to Find, Enjoy, and Keep Real Love (A Common-Sense Guide to a Healthy Relationship).*

©2010, 2015, 2016 & 2018 by J. B. Love.

ISBN: Softcover 978-0-9971875-4-0
ISBN: E-book 978-0-9971875-5-7

www.jblovebooks.com

This book was edited by Bella Love and Ruby Watford
This book was printed in the United States of America

Disclaimer

This book is a guide to maximizing your potential in a business and personal setting to live a balanced life on your terms. The author wrote about her education, the experiences in her life, the advice she received, and the actions she observed. The discussions in this book are things she has seen work or fail consistently over the years. It is worth the read. The author is pluralistic and respects the differences in races and religions. She feels that we all belong to "the human race," and her humanity is as such. Although she speaks about the doctrine of her faith, she understands that there is sound doctrine found in other religions as well.

The sale of this book by the author and publisher is not rendering psychological, financial, legal, or other professional services. Any application of the material in the following pages is at the reader's discretion and sole responsibility.

The author and publisher have made every effort to ensure that the information in this book was correct at press time. The author and publisher do not assume and hereby disclaim any liability to any party for any reason.

CONTENTS

ACKNOWLEDGMENT

To all the people that made this project possible,
I acknowledge and thank you.

A world without color would be a world without you.
May you continue to inspire me to
paint my world a masterpiece.

A Mind of Many Colors

My mind is of many colors, each shade is unique.
Like a box of crayons, when put together this
makes my mindset complete.
With my mind of many colors, the world is my
canvas and I am the artist for all to see,
As I continue to reach beyond the stars, to paint
my world a masterpiece.

J. B. Love

DEDICATION

I dedicate this book to all the dreamers, doers, way makers, risk takers, and result getters of the world. Don't be afraid to fly even if it's alone. May you continue to dream and think big, plan, prepare, act, persist positively and succeed beyond your wildest dreams and imagination. If you are reading this, that means YOU! There will be infinite possibilities and opportunities if you do. Always remember to:

L
W I N
V
L I F E

Live Life & Win

INTRODUCTION

If you're looking for the perfect motivation, inspiration and empowerment book you have reached the right designation by choosing *Think Big, Achieve BIGGER (The Little Black Book of Success in the Workplace and Life)*. The road to success begins with a BIG idea. You just made one by purchasing this book. In this book, you will learn how to think BIG no matter what your circumstances are in life. Like her other books, *Anticipation, 10 Keys to Turning Your Dreams into Reality, Love, Life and Courage (Poetry for the Soul), and How to Keep and Find Real Love (A Common-Sense Guide to a Healthy Relationship)*, this book looks at the author's journey on her road to success on her terms. You will learn how she makes a lemon cake out of lemons in life.

J. B. Love is a results-getter with a proven track record. She has saved organizations millions of dollars during her career and received numerous promotions within a short period after joining an organization. Therefore, she knows how to think BIG and achieve BIGGER and wants to share that with the world.

Everyone desires success, but not everyone is willing to do what it takes to obtain it, keep it, or have it on their terms. Thank you for purchasing this valuable resource tool. Now, turn the pages and get started on your journey to elevate yourself and obtain success on your terms.

Think Beyond Boundaries
Think BIG Acronym

Think Beyond Current Limits as Thoughts Are Powerful

Have a Plan, Prepare, Act, & Persist Positively

Imagine "Possible"

Never Give Up or Become Too Complacent

Know Dreams Can Be Turned into Reality &
Success Awaits You

Be Your Best Self

Involve Your Dream Team *(Together Everyone Achieve More)*

Grow as Greater and Bigger Achievements Are
Inevitable

*Greater are they that see the "Big Picture" Then
Plan, Prepare, Act, & Persist Accordingly.*

CHAPTER 1

There Is Power in Thoughts

The road to success begins with a BIG idea. Thoughts are powerful. They drive our will and rule our actions. You need to think beyond your current boundaries. If you don't, you will never be able to rise above your current situation. The bigger the thought, the bigger the achievement if you plan, prepare, act, and put the right plans into motion.

The great poet, Maya Angelou once said, "if your dreams don't scare you, they are not big enough." If you dream of small things, you achieve small things. You can only achieve what your mind has conceived. Michelangelo was a man of great vision. His painting of the Sistine Chapel ceiling is amazing. If you are not familiar with this work of art, go to your local library or your favorite search engine and look up "Michelangelo's Sistine Chapel ceiling" and go to Wikipedia, the free online encyclopedia. According to Wikipedia, he was initially only commissioned to paint the 12 Apostles against a starry sky. However, Michelangelo had a different vision. The work turned out to be unbelievable. Like Michelangelo, you should always reach for the stars and beyond.

Keeping a Positive Mindset

It is difficult to "Think BIG" if you are not positive or relaxed. That is why it is essential to stay positive. The truth is if you tell yourself you cannot do something chances are you will never act to put the things in motion that are needed to achieve that goal. I stay positive by repeating or writing positive affirmations. I avoid negativity. I listen to music, smile, and laugh by watching comedians. Smiling and laughing has benefits:

SMILING

Reduces stress levels

Retrains the brain to think positive

Helps with weight-loss

Makes you more approachable

Smiling and laughing releases chemicals in the brain that makes you feel happy and reduces stress levels. The more these chemicals are released, the happier and more relaxed you feel. It is the body's natural painkiller. It lowers your stress hormone. So, smile and unleash the happiness within.

Never look for happiness in others which can leave you feeling alone. Instead, smile and find joy in yourself which will leave you feeling happy even when you are alone.

Always think of the possibilities in life. There is possible in "imPOSSIBLE." If you believe you can, with the right plan, preparation, actions, and persistence, you will. Persistence is important. Although you may have to modify your plans, you should never give up. You become what you believe and do consistently. We become our visions. You are what you repeat.

Strategies for Thinking BIG

Throughout my life two strategies gave birth to new ideas:

1. A need or problem and it's solution
2. Rising above circumstances

Want a BIG opportunity? Find a BIG problem. Your thoughts need to fulfill a need or solve a problem. Marketable products and services are born out of attempts to satisfy a need or to solve a problem. It does not do you any good beyond your satisfaction to invent what you think is the best product or service in the world if there is no need for it or it does not have mass or the right appeal. Therefore, you should center your thoughts on a need or a problem solution.

You should keep a journal of your thoughts and ideas. Sometimes we forget ideas that pop into our minds. By doing this, you will be amazed at how it will save you time, and you will never lose those big ideas. Over the years I would scribble my thoughts in a diary or on paper if I was in public at the time of there origination. If I were alone, I would speak them into an electronic device. Later in life, I put together books based on them. For example, the "Love" section of "Love, Life, and Courage *(Poetry for the Soul)*" contains numerous poems I wrote for my now husband when we were dating that we kept. Therefore, when people ask me how do I write an entire book in weeks, my reply is, "I've been writing this journey my entire life."

I had many obstacles and circumstances to overcome: First, I had to relocate a time or two because my spouse was in the military. Except for those organizations that had a branch in the new location I was moving to, it meant starting over again and again. Second, I was a female and a minority which came with its own set of unique challenges and circumstances. I never let either of these things stop me. I would look at those circumstances to find the opportunities in them and rose above them. Often, what others mean for your bad can turn into your good if you make it so. There is an old concept of "making lemons out of lemonade." However, in my case, instead of only making lemonade, I thought big and made a lemon cake as well.

Get Your Promotion

When you seek to find the opportunities in your circumstances, that is when you will rise. In thinking big, you should learn to work smarter and not harder. In corporate America and the world, it is all about the bottom line. You must think how can the unique set of skills that you have to bring to the table help the organization's "bottom line" in money, time or image. Just because others have always done things a certain way, does not mean it's the most efficient or best way. I'm not talking about re-inventing a perfect wheel. I am merely referring to optimization to free up time and resources for those tasks that need it.

Need/Problem/Solution Theory

I have always thought BIG. It may be easier than you think. Now, I am going to talk about what I call my *"Need/Problem/Solution Theory"* to thinking BIG. Big thoughts for me have always been born out of a need/problem and solution to those needs/problems.

For me, it began in college. From the beginning, I had the bigger picture in mind. Because I was working full-time and going to school full-time, I had limited time. I always sought to automate redundant tasks to save time. It placed me ahead of the game and propelled my career. I was taking an accounting class where we had accounting problems for class work and homework:

Problem: Limited time to handwrite redundant classwork and homework spreadsheets and calculate them. The course did not have a companion workbook. If there were one, the accounts would not have been written down for you, and you would still have had to use a calculator.

Solution: Big Thought: Develop an electronic accounting spreadsheet for myself to save time: Bigger Thought: Sell it to others.

Every college paper I wrote, I did so with a final thesis in mind. Therefore, when I was in my last year of graduate school six years later 75% of my thesis was already done. When I graduated, I graduated ranked #1 in my undergraduate class among all majors and received a fellowship to graduate school. Also, to use my time wisely, my thesis was based on a problem at one of the organization's I was working for so I "killed two birds with one stone" so to speak.

Success in the business world was similar. The following are some problems and solutions from my work experiences:

When I was a contract advertising auditor for a major national/international newspaper, in my first three months of employment, I saved the organization over $300,000 plus and cut the number of advertising rate adjustments by 50% the next year:

Problem: Staff was making numerous adjustments to multi-million-dollar retail advertising accounts after billing. Coding was problematic as the codes didn't relate to anything other than vacant numbers. No one in the Management Information Systems *(MIS)* department knew anything about Accounting, and when they talked to someone in Accounting, they couldn't convey what they needed to do their job as a user of a nationwide computerized accounting program.

Solution: Big Thought: Save the company time and money while making my job easier. Bigger Thought: Propel me into a new career. Develop a relatable rate code table so that the accounts could be coded correctly based on the advertising contract that was signed by the retailer. Update codes in the MIS database. Train staff on the new codes and salespeople on the benefits *(cost-*

saving) of retailer's signing larger contracts for a better rate and run a test billing before billing to catch any errors. Because I developed it, it was easy for me to memorize the rate table itself. Results: $300,000 plus savings. I went to this organization as an accounting clerk. Within a year, I was functioning as a Senior Business Systems Analyst for new accounting software releases worldwide and became a District Manager.

When I was an executive for another International Organization, I automated basic training courses, computerized resources, and got rid of numerous computer contracts. It cut the organization's computer services expense by 80% and increased the number of volunteers able to receive training by 100% within the first week of implementation. The organization had two major problems:

Problem 1: In the case of the training & recognition, the organization had four significant issues:

1. Not enough volunteer trainers and volunteer leaders.
2. Volunteers did not have time to attend the number of classes required to become certified within a reasonable timeframe.
3. No training tracking software for staff and volunteers.

4. No streamlined recognition process was resulting in not having enough staff and time to sort through hundreds of application requests across the state.

Solution: My thought process was, "Why do we require the volunteers to physically have to come to a site to learn basic information and why do all the recognition applications look the same? Develop audio, online, and color-coded correspondence courses for basic training so that volunteers could complete the course on their own time and do not have to come and physically sit in a class. Purchase and implement a training management software for staff and volunteers that would automatically alert you when certified training *(i.e., CPR and First Aid &, etc.)* was expiring. Color code the different types of recognition so that when they came into the office, staff could put them in the appropriate locked boxes without having to read the application to determine what recognition the person was sending the volunteer for review. Also, every application/form &, etc. was placed on a disk and online. Because it was more cost-effective, took less time and was more convenient to become certified, they had all the basic things for their meeting. Volunteerism and the organization's image increased.

Pay Attention to details. The BIGGEST impact is often found in the smallest details.

You must pay attention to the details. Something as simple as color-coding items made the biggest impact. For example, the organization had different colors for its levels; therefore, by making the correspondence courses covers to match the different levels, you automatically knew which level training it was for by eyesight alone. The staff could now pull them off the shelf without having to read it. It worked the same for the recognition.

Problem 2: In the case of information technology (IT), the organization had two significant issues:

1. Outsourcing IT for simple IT functions.
2. Not conducting audits and depreciating assets.

Solution: 1: My thought was why are we outsourcing all our information technology needs when we have a technology staff in-house. The in-house staff that was assigned the computer responsibility knew hardly anything about computer technology, but since the agency did not either, they had no clue. The technology company the agency was using was not going to tell them any better as they were making megabucks off this company. I discovered this when I presented a list of technology needs to the Executive Director *(ED)* that should have been basic, and the ED told me the computer person said it was not doable. The services that the organization was outsourcing could be done in-house if the staff was qualified. The current staff who was responsible for IT was an administrative assistant that knew how to do word processing and could make phone calls to the contracted IT company. I did my research, presented my cost/benefit analysis and was approved to implement. It was a cost saving of more than 60%.

Solution 2: The accounting person was also the ED's office at the time and said you should have half the things you asked for because they were on the balance sheet. I merely asked her; when was the last time that you conducted an audit? They said never. When I offered to conduct an audit, and the ED agreed, this is what I discovered. This organization not only did not conduct audits they did not depreciate anything. They merely were carrying the assets from year to year at purchase value with no depreciation. Therefore, their listed assets were not correct. Part of them was missing, and the other half were obsolete. When I finished helping them correct their accounting, they were in the hole to the tune of approximately $100,000.

BIGGER picture: I was initially hired by this organization as an Adult Services Manager but ended up becoming Director of Adult Services and Information Technology. When I went to the Board of Directors luncheon and the ED reported on the cost-savings and new findings. The president of the board of directors asked how much of these savings would I benefit from regarding a salary increase and that is how I received a promotion that came with a sizable increase in pay.

My biggest cost-saving regarding money was over Two million *($2,000,0000)* dollars when I worked for another organization when I discover their fiscal year budget was off by over $2,000,000 just before them sending it to the state Senate for approval in the legislature. In this organization system, I received three promotions within two years.

My "Need/Problem/Solution" Theory can work for your better. I never complained about a problem that I could not provide a solution for or put together a task group to solve. I was always seeking to "make a lemon cake out of lemonade."

I know that there are authors out there that will tell people that "It not what you know, but who you know." However, this only works when you are trying to get your foot in the door or trying to get a promotion initially. The bigger picture is to keep the job or promotions, and for that, you will need "what you know." In all my years of working, I know of none who got to keep their job or promotion who did not have the skills after the person that gave them their position left the organization. A diversified set of skills and proven track record matters in the bigger picture of things. What separated me from others was that I was not one-dimensional, and I did not get my job based solely on who I knew. Like education, "who you know" *get you in the door, but diversification, flexibility, people skills & character elevates and keeps you there.* When I went to college, on the advice of my brother, I chose to major in Business Management because you need management in every field that exists. I then decided to take computer science/technology and accounting classes for every elective, later returning to get an associate degree in computer technology. One way to get ahead is to become diversified. The other important thing is that again; I never complained about a problem unless I had a solution.

Who Moved My Comfort Zone?

However, change sometimes comes with opposition. Many of the people in the organizations I worked for had what I call the "Who Moved My Comfort Zone" syndrome. We all know there is safety in comfort zones, but nothing ever grows there. The people that reside in the comfort zone I will refer to as "comfortees." Every one of these comfortees had attended workshops on the *'Who Moved My Cheese* book, but very few could apply it to their real-life situations. It was as if they attended it merely because it was popular, everyone was doing it, or they wanted to get away from work, etc. They did not recognize themselves in the characters; therefore, there was no ownership and no desire to change. Also, they were never held accountable for their actions. Unless you hold people accountable for their actions they will never get it. There was a system broken where employees could thrive in a bad way. The organization should have written some employees up or fired them for their behavior, but they did not. "Comfortees" are comfortable doing what they have done in the past and will not welcome change or the person helping to implement the change. It is always good to include people in changes; however, from real life experiences, you must realize that sometimes, it will not matter whether you include them in a task group or not. It was not their idea, and they are not going to support it. The "comfortees" will not be willing to change and will make you a target. The textbooks in college do not go into full details about being a target in the workplace to prepare you better. Since I graduated college, maybe they have added a course that has dedicated a semester to addressing serious issues in the workplace. Sure, there are classes on Business Ethics; however, when I was in college, there were not any seminar classes that prepared you for survival in the "rat race."

There are monsters in this world, and some of them are human and work in the workplace throughout all levels of employment.

In the real world, there are horrible things that occur in the workplace. Things like:

Professional Sabotage *(Modern-Day Witch Hunts)*

Pressure to Participate in Illegal Activities.

Violence in the Workplace and Death Threats

Criminal Sexual Misconduct

From my experience in the workplace, I feel that universities need to offer a semester class where you can roleplay the above situations just like they do work teams in a senior level Management Seminar class. Usually, they cover these subjects only briefly. I was young when I started out, and my education did not prepare me for all the horrible things that happen to me at a young adult age.

I will talk about different scenario throughout this book but will offer some of my tips for the above that are good practices:

- **Always do your best.** No matter what someone else will ever say about you, your work will always speak for itself.

- **Stay ethical and moral even when others are not.** Staying ethical and moral is important because it will work better for you in the long run. It was never about my relationship with any of them but my relationship with GOD.

- **Document, Document, Document.** I can't say this enough. The best way to document is with e-mails and read-receipt, cc: function, and text messages. The e-mails should be professional, but it should bring up the issue: *i.e., "To foster teamwork," etc. "I appreciate the work you do in helping our organization serve our, etc." "I love my job., but lately there has not been teamwork, etc.".* I even documented the departmental training I gave my staff. I did so because when you must write an employee up for not doing their job, the first defense they will give is, "You did not train me properly" or that you are harassing them. That is hard to say when they have signed off on departmental training and have open read receipt e-mails warning them for their behavior or performance and offering further training. Trust me when push comes to shove you will need these e-mails.

- **Report events when they happen by e-mail or company complaint systems.** You also need to identify the specific company policy or practice that the employee violated. You may not think so, but most time your haters have already been reporting you falsely to upper management directly or indirectly.

- **Pay attention to your gut feelings or intuition.** There is something in business management that refers to relying on your gut feeling. My gut feelings have always served me well. If you feel something is wrong, chances are there is something wrong. Simply put, *check it out first and if it doesn't feel right, be prepared to take flight (remove yourself from the situation).*

- **Never participate in illegal activity.** Your supervisor and employer can't force you to commit or help commit a crime. Report such requests immediately in writing to your superiors. If your superiors request the same, resign and move to your next blessing. Keep the written report and the answer. Although it is not a lot of money, you will be able to collect unemployment while looking for a new job.

- **Never participate or tolerate violence in the workplace.** Report immediately. If your organization plays it off, file a grievance if your organization has this process. Be prepared to call 911 if necessary or for your safety move on. You may think I am over thinking here, but I received two death threats in my career. In both cases, the organization's representative played it off like it was nothing. I talked about one in this book when I reported sexual harassment to my then employer, and the other was where an employee I supervised was facing termination.

- **After you have gathered evidence** *(e-mails, witnesses, recordings, &, etc.)*, **report sexual harassment when it occurs in writing.** If it is reported verbally first, follow up in writing *(e-mail w/ read receipt)*. Ask for a meeting with your superiors in writing and say that it is about sexual harassment. I would not put it in the subject line but in the e-mail itself. Some superiors are cleaver in not opening e-mail of certain topics to say they never received an e-mail from you; therefore, you never reported it. I once had a supervisor who was the head of human resources who told me to stop sending e-mails because people did not like them. I would print a copy of the read-receipt for your records. If your organization does nothing about the issue, I would report it to the Equal Employment Opportunity Commission *(EEOC)*; however, time is of the essence for filing claims of discrimination or retaliation. I would check with the organization for the deadline information. A word of caution. Only report if your claim is true. I worked in human resources, and I am aware of false claims that were not true. Some employees participated in affairs with co-workers then cried sexual harassment when they did not get what they wanted, and others never had an affair. They simply did not get what they wanted and cried wolf. These can get you a trip to the unemployment line or worse.

- **Know when it's time to move on.** Sometimes in life one door closes so you can open another. You should always stay marketable and keep your ears and eyes open for better opportunities elsewhere. Only you know when you have had enough. It is important that you pay attention to the signs around you. If you do, you can usually tell when your employer is seeking to replace you. You do not have to do anything wrong for this to happen. Sometimes when top positions change, they want to bring in the people they know and trust. Also, you don't want to end up in a dead-end job that you hate and have stayed there for twenty years still complaining and crying at your desk for others to hear and see. I once worked with a lady who had this problem.

- **Beware of the honeymoon phase.** This phase usually occurs during an employee's probationary period. During this time, you may think everything seems perfect, but you can't let your guard down. When the honeymoon phase is over that is when things usually become heated. Sometimes the employee appears to change drastically.

> *Sometimes it's not people who change.*
> *They stop pretending, then the mask*
> *falls off and reveals their true self.*

I once had an employee who was a poser *(pretending to be someone she was not)*. Somehow, she thought she was in a permanent employee identification number as opposed to a non-permanent, at-will number. She waited until she felt her probationary period was over and began to help sabotage my department on the promise of promotion from one of the "comfortees." It did not work out for either of them. They took their scheme a little too far. I made it a habit never to burn bridges. I kept a relationship with the human resource department after I decided it was time to move on to my current position in this scenario at this organization. I would visit the director for short periods sometimes on breaks even though my gut feelings told me he was part of the problem. While I was in his office one day, the "comfortee" who was another executive at the organization placed a call to him and sent him an urgent e-mail where she referred to me as a tyrant. She said that he needed to get the employee away from me as I was down in the department right now doing XYZ. In the e-mail or phone call, she said I am causing the employee to have health conditions &, etc. We caught them. Talk about *"Liar, Liar Pants on Fire."* Well, I was sitting in the HR director's office at the time. You see, they would never have thought I would have kept a business relationship with a man I once had to report. A man who had told me on different occasions, *"You better not tell anyone."* With me, it was always about business and never personal. Sometimes you must beat people at their own game. There is a saying about keeping your enemies close. To a degree, it implies in the business world as well. It is hard for someone to participate in a witch-hunt against you for harassment of anybody when every time you wrote an employee up for violations of policies they signed off on the paperwork. In the end, it was the "comfortee" who e-mailed me and told me to terminate the employee. I had a gut feeling about the "comfortee," and when several department heads tipped me off to them, my gut feeling was validated. These were women who on the surface pretending to like me. However, the knives that were stuck so deep in my back hurt. It was so bad that one of the department heads that warned me told me the "comfortee" was dangerous and that I better not tell anyone, or she would ruin me as she has that kind of power. They told me she will not get caught doing it but will have someone else do it. She is that clever. An echo from the past that was resurfacing. It was like it was straight out of Alice Walker's *The Color Purple novel*, "You better not never tell nobody but God." and at that moment I felt just like the 14-year-old abused child from that story. I did not know whether it was her warning me or that was the threat itself, and I did not care. At the right time, I told the right people. I kept calm and waited until they played their hand first. Thing got worse before it was over. It was here that I received one of two death threats in the workplace. Every day I entered that building I would repeat *Psalms 23: 4 - 6* from the King James Version of *The Bible*:

Yea, though I walk through the valley of the shadow of death. I will fear no evil: for thou art with me: thy rod and thy staff they comfort me. Thou preparest a table before me in the presence of mine enemies: thou anointest my head with oil; my cup runneth over. Surely goodness and mercy shall follow me all the days of my life . . .

Dealing with "comfortees" in the workplace can be difficult. You must have the right people *(Executive Directors, Presidents, and Board of Directors)* in organizations behind you. You will need this if you are a "Game Changer." I am not saying it will be easy; however, it will be necessary for growth. Growth does not occur with things staying the same. Change must occur, and you must be committed to the goals. There is nothing meek and mild about being an innovator, leader or a game changer if you are to be successful. You must be willing to take calculated risks. Sometimes, it will be necessary to move on. Too much stress can be the downfall of your health, and it is not worth the risk. It doesn't pay to win the battle but lose the war.

I must say this about skills and accomplishments. You should never pad them especially if you cannot back them up. Either my supervisor or I documented all my accomplishment in my evaluations. If the organization did not put them there when they did part one of my reviews, in my response to the review I made sure I did. I simply told how I loved my job and the organization and how I appreciated the help in saving our organization XYZ which would allow us to serve our customer and community better. I made the accomplishments about how we as a team can better serve the customer and community; thereby, increase the company's image.

The BIGGER picture is that an organization cares less about you receiving more money than they care about their bottom line and image.

Above the other attributes that I possess, my *"Need/Problem/Solution Theory"* has always elevated and propelled me to the next level in life. This only works in organizations with upward movement. If you have been at an organization for years and nothing is wrong with your image or skills, and you have made numerous valuable contributions and have not gotten a promotion or reward, this is where you may need to move on. I went into an organization and got my first promotion at nine months, followed by my second one six months later, then the third one shortly after that. To get the promotions, I had to move from one area of the organization to the next. For growth, your comfort zone must continually expand beyond its boundaries.

I believe in the power of thought. I remind myself often; especially when life hands me unpleasant circumstances. It is like a voice in my head reminding me of what I need to do to overcome and excel. It's my way of living life and winning. Here is my think BIG chant:

Think BIG

You got to think big.
You can't think small.
You got to think big.
Life is not a dance but a ball.
You got to think big.
Not short but tall.
You got to think big
or you might miss your call.
You got to think big
when your back is against the wall.
You got to think big
whether you stand or fall.
You got to think big
not short-term but a long haul.
You got to think big
if you want to have it all.

There is power in thoughts.
They drive our will and rule our actions.
If you think small things,
you achieve small things.

Unlock Your Dreams
We Become Our Visions
We Are What We Repeat

Determination *(Our dedications to our beliefs)*

Responsibility *(The duty we have to ourselves and others)*

Education *(Knowledge, both formal and informal)*

Action *(The gap between imagination and realization)*

Motivation *(The driving force of our actions)*

Success *(Our rewards for our persistent actions)*

Dream & Think BIG,
Plan, Prepare, Act, Persist, Elevate,
Succeed, Repeat &
Live Your Dreams!
Acronym taken from J. B. Love's
Anticipation, 10 Keys to Turning Your Dreams into Reality
available on www.amazon.com

CHAPTER 2

Be Your Best Self

Your first product is yourself. Are you marketable? If you are not, unless you are lucky, I don't see "Achieving Bigger" in your situation. Your best self would be knowledge and keep up with the ever-changing dynamics in your field and network if you are to survive, elevate yourself, and not get left behind. You are marketable if you are up-to-date on:

Your skills and industry knowledge
Your education, certification, and training
Your networking and communication activities
Your image *(character, clothes, hair, &, etc.)*
Your balance between your life and work

The above are the basics. They will get you in the door. However, you will need the following types of things that will keep you there and propel to the next level:

> Think Big, Positive Mind-Set
> Confidence
> Diversified Skills Set
> Dependability
> Flexibility
> Ability to Work Smarter
> Results Getter Track Record
> Interpersonal Skills
> Business Ethics
> Avoid Gossip
> Involvement in ORG's Activities
> Never Become Complacent

Before you can achieve anything, you must first learn to love, to be, and to believe in yourself. I am not talking about obnoxious, outrageous arrogance. I am talking about confidence. Low self-esteem and surviving the rat race is not a good combination. There is simply a prince or princess in all of us who can if prepared, achieve anything our mind can conceive; however, we must first look inside ourselves to find and be them. Sometimes the naysayers in our lives try to block us from our blessings and are a hindrance to us in seeing all the possibilities within ourselves. Recognizing who these naysayers are, ignoring their negative nonconstructive talk, and removing ourselves from their toxic world can make a world of difference.

Sometimes this naysayer is our self. Yes, we often hinder ourselves. You must learn that sometimes you have to:

Tell the negative voice in your head to "get somewhere, sit down, and be quiet because you are on a mission of success and there is no room for negativity occupying valuable real estate in your head."

Be confident in who you are and, in your abilities, and it will shine through. The Wright brothers had to love and believe in their selves; people probably thought they were crazy as they traveled on their road to turning their *dream (a flying machine that we now call the airplane)* into reality. We should celebrate differences; however, most people do not. They do not or do not want to understand anything different than themselves, especially if it was not their idea. Just think about it. If no one had ever been different, we all would still be living in caves chiseling out picture messages on rocks. *Without diversity, there is no growth.* Don't worry, if you prepare yourself, you will shine when your time comes.

Embrace your uniqueness. When I was younger, I too did not understand why I was different. Because I was extremely skinny, people used to pick at me by calling me hurtful names. My thought process was very different as well. I spent a lot of time alone drawing, writing things, designing and sewing purses & clothes, and listening to and singing along with my favorite music. I had dreams of becoming an entertainer, model or fashion designer. My friends had all the popular boyfriends while the boys were my friends *(I was a tomboy who participated in sports)*. I felt bad that none of them saw me as a girlfriend type. They mostly treated me as not pretty enough or fine enough. However, I went on to become a model, a businesswoman, recording artist & author. You see, you must love and believe in yourself enough to ignore people when they mean you no good. It doesn't matter if your first attempt was unsuccessful. Always remember that pitfalls in life are just stepping-stones to something great if we learn from our mistakes, get back up, and try again. Now, I look back and smile. I finally realized that all the pitfalls I experienced were helping me to become who I am today. That is why I always say you should look for the opportunities in your circumstances. They are there. I know when you are hurting, you don't see them. But if you keep moving and make the right choices, things will work out for you.

As mentioned earlier, I had to relocate several times because my husband was in the military. For me, it was an opportunity to expand my education, volunteer, meet new people, and learn the new area's customs and practices. I joined professional networking groups which led to new opportunities for me. I went from a young lady in a small town where I was allowing others to make me feel like an outcast to being accepted in the bigger world out there. The best business advice I ever got came from a German businessman while networking, a mid-western businessman while at a July 4th barbeque, and a team of headhunters on the west coast. Notice how all these venues were different.

I had to learn to be my best self. It was key to my survival in my ever-changing world. Beside the location changes, I encountered several obstacles in the workplace and my personal life. Someone even suggested to me that I "dumb down" so people would like me more. There is enough crazy stuff in my diary for a novel. Before I became injured, I never let any of it stop me. I was determined not to let anything anyone did to me change me. It's like Swindoll says: *Life is 10% of what happens to you and 90% how you react to it.*

Knowing the difference between education and intelligence is key to being your best self. Education speaks to knowledge. It is you knowing what to say. Intelligence speaks to the application of knowledge. It is you knowing when and how to say it or if it should be said at all. Being intelligent is essential to interpersonal skills, networking, and success. Success does not occur in a vacuum. It is vital in your personal and professional relationships that you be able to get along with others. The most educated people are not necessarily the most successful people. We all know of people who are very educated but are not very intelligent. They are the ones that know everything, and you can't tell them anything. Conversations with them are a struggle. Their interpersonal skills are not good at all as their conversations are usually onesided as they do not relate any of their replies to the topic at hand. They are only listening to hear so they can respond. Before long, you will be in an argument with them about something. You should never argue with someone who only wants to win a fight and not learn anything. You must listen, ask questions to get an understanding and do your research if necessary about a person or subject matter before giving your opinion. Here are the signs people are listening:

- They hear what you say and have a relevant reply. *(Listen, and Silent have the same letters)*.
- They don't sigh or interrupt your flow of speaking so they can talk about what they want to say.
- You received what you asked of them.

Although people are unique, here are some essential traits of intelligent people:

- They are approachable and active listeners.
- They remember names, patterns & processes.
- They can learn quickly and adapt to changes.

- They are their best self and can apply knowledge.
- They are open-minded but never gives in to any and everything because it's a fad or popular.
- They never become complacent and grow continually.
- They are curious and unafraid to ask questions and take calculated risks.
- They learn from mistakes. *(If it happens more than once, it not a mistake it's a choice.)*
- They are self-reliant regarding positivity and resources.
- They know when they are ignorant about a subject matter and listens or seek to learn more.
- They base their opinions on facts.
- They have empathy and compassion.

It is never too late to make a change. Know that your caterpillar days will not last forever if you start.

Staying drug-free is a major key to be your best self and thinking BIG. There is absolutely no way you can achieve and maintain greatness if your mind is not at its best. Drugs are traps. They impair your mind's ability to think and reason. Not to mention all the money you will waste on them. Natural highs are free, and they leave your mind intact with the ability to generate new BIG ideas, process information, and make good decisions. Drugs are a robber of dreams and wealth. Stay drug-free.

Win BIG by Choosing Right

Rocky or smooth the paths on the roads of life
we choose,
Always determines whether we win or lose.
Right, wrong or popular the decision is ours to
make;
However, it takes more effort to clean up
mistakes.
So, make good choices and make them well.
If you choose the right path, you're sure to
elevate and excel.

Every choice we make in life leads us to our destiny.
What will your destiny be? Choose Right.

<u>Share Love Equally</u>

You cannot confine beauty to certain races.
You cannot determine people's character by their
faces.
Crazy, ignorance and an ugly heart know no skin
color or spaces.
Don't miss out on life's blessings by only looking in
certain places.

CHAPTER 3

Win BIG by Choosing Right

*W*in big by choosing right. You always win or lose by what you choose. Doing the right thing the first time will save you a lot of time and money. It is harder to correct mistakes made from bad decisions than to get it right the first time. Our decisions lead us to our destiny. Your failure or success will depend upon the paths you choose in life.

Choosing Right

Stay Focused. Having a clear vision will help you recognize which dream is worth chasing. According to Confucius, "The man who chases two rabbits catches neither." Keeping your focus is key. Time is valuable. Once it is gone, you can never get it back. It's like water that passes through a stream. You must choose the right people, opportunities, product or service to invest your time. *Opportunities will come, and some may go, but the right ones you choose will add to your glow.* Choosing the right opportunity for you, will start your growth and make it enjoyable. In this section, I will discuss products and services. Of the millions of dollars spent each year on developing new products only a few make it to the marker and fewer enjoy a long shelf life. Just like the thought process, as I mentioned earlier, a product or service should meet a need, want, or solve a problem. You should ask three questions:

1. Does it meet a need, want, or solve a problem? If it is not a solution to one of the above, it will never have mass appeal.

2. Will it have mass appeal? It must be appealing to more than yourself and close family members and friends unless that is your attention.

3. Is it unique? If the market already has the same product and yours is no different, why would someone buy yours? Can you offer the same quality of product or better at a lower price than the competition? If not, they are not likely to buy it.

You can look up all the inventions inventors filed a patent for, and the products failed, and you will see why the above is important.

I compiled writings I did over the years for my books. Except for the papers, I wrote when I was in college., I did not know that I would be compiling books years later. I initially created handouts to be used in the workshops I conducted in organizations, universities, and churches. However, I started getting calls from people requesting copies. The first book I wrote I used a publisher. The process to me was horrible; the book contains numerous errors even though they said that they used an editor and I created most of the work myself including artwork. They received most of the profit; therefore, I formed my own publishing imprint company to publish the rest of my books and had them printed. It was born out of my need to have my work published and not get ripped off. I already had the skills needed. I had the education. I was already functioning as a desktop publisher and web designer when I started my desktop publishing and website company.

I started this company when I was between jobs. I was volunteering and serving as the Vice-President of Communication for the local chapter of the American Society for Training and Development where I became President-elect. One of my responsibilities was to maintain their website and publish a monthly newsletter. I started it after the compliment of a print house executive after viewing some of my work who told me it was some of the most brilliant he had seen. He said it was better than any of the work they were getting from the big advertising agencies in the area. The BIG idea was born that I could do this for myself. Why not? I was saving organizations big dollars doing the same type work. Just as I did, you can do it also.

Where I lived at the time, I could offer a better-quality service at a much cheaper cost because I did not have a huge overhead. The start-up cost would be minimal as I could operate the business from home then write it off as an expense on my taxes for operating a business out of my home.

After the doctor diagnosed me with cancer, I ended that company and referred the clients, and while thinking what else that I could do that would not be so taxing on me, that is when I remembered all the different types of writing I had done over the years in good time and bad times.

It was as if God said, "I have given you everything you need to survive and succeed. It's been within you all along. You just need to recognize it and get started".

Out of this BIG idea, I started to put together some of my writing for my first book. That experience led to my frustration with the publisher which led me to publish my books. Because I needed an imprint name for the block of ISBN numbers I purchased, that led to the birth of J. B. Love Books, the publishing imprint for J. B. Love, the American author, recording artist, and poet. I now have my fourth book. I have enough material from over the years to put out several more books on various subjects. My belief in God has always gotten me through tough times.

People have different hobbies. Maybe there is something that you have been doing that could fulfill a need, want or solve a problem that is marketable. There is an old saying *"Nothing beats a failure but a try."* You will never know unless you prepare and act on the idea. Whatever you choose, it must be something that you have a passion for and not someone else's passion or skills. Often people look at others who are successful at something, and they decide if they did it, it must be easy, so they spend their time trying to recreate someone else's dream. If you choose right, your journey will be enjoyable.

Learn to keep secrets of projects before you launch them to yourself. Always copyright and seek patents for your works and inventions that are original ideas before someone else steals your idea for their own. Write the character and words on your work *(i.e., ©2010 by Jane/John Doe. All Rights Reserved).*

You can register your copyright by going to www.copyright.gov. The cheapest and quickest way to submit is electronically. There will be a fee for each application you register. When I was younger and did not have the money for the registration fee just yet, I copyrighted my materials and used the poor man's copyright method. I made a copy first then put my copyrighted work into an envelope and mailed it to myself. I didn't open it when I received it. Once I got the funds, I proceeded with the registration process. You should note that this method in legal terms has no real standing as it relates to copyrights because anyone can fake copyright; however, doing something is better than nothing. However, it stopped some of my ambitious associates who attempted to swipe a few pages of my work to use as their own. When they learned that I did this, I stopped hearing what they had written among other associates. It is best to copyright your material by putting it on your work and registering it with the United States Copyright Office as soon as you can.

If you are an inventor, and it's a patent you seek, visit the website www.uspto.gov. You can find answers to many of your questions that are related to patents. History has shown us over the years who invented products as opposed to those who took or tried to take credit for creating them.

Creations in the workplace work a little different. We know that people steal ideas all the time and make them their own. However, in the business world, you must keep in mind "Intellectual Property." If you created something during your employment as defined by your job duties and done in the ordinary course of your duties, your employer owns the intellectual property rights to that creation. Especially if your employer directed the activities that led to the creation. Employers are very smart, and most employment job duty descriptions and contracts contain statements regarding intellectual property. Therefore, most creations on company time belong to the company.

Nevertheless, safeguard your work before another employee takes credit for it and get the promotion that you deserve and probably would have gotten. However, some employers do offer pay for ideas that save them time and money. I worked for a supplier of a major manufacturing company that paid their employees for cost saving ideas.

Again, it is imperative to understand which idea is worth investing all your time, energy and money. Your goal is to grow. As mentioned earlier in this book, for growth, change is necessary, and you must commit to your goals. You want to be unique, but, there must be a need and a want for your product or service if you are to survive beyond product development. You should act on your ideas. You have uniqueness within you and can make an impact. The next time you feel that you can't make an impact in the world remember that the giant corporation, Apple, was started by two college dropouts in one of their parent's garage. Now, how is that for thinking big and achieving bigger.

The Three Vital "Cs" of Growth

Your growth will depend on your ability to:

Choose Right if you want to start & enjoy growth.
Change if needed if you want to continue growing.
Commit if you want to elevate your growth.

DREAMS + CONTINUED ACTION = REALITY
ACTION − PREPARATION = DISASTER

Build a Dream Team & Invest in Them

Who's on your Dream Team? Surround yourself with greatness: Your dream team or inner circle should be people who uplift, empower, inspire, motivate and are smarter than you as it is the only way to grow.

CHAPTER 4

Plan, Prepare and Act

ction is the master key to all success. Now that you have chosen right, it time to act on your dreams. It is the only way to turn them into realities. Everyone has dreams, but not everyone acts on them. Simply Do Something. You must stop dreaming and start doing for your dreams to come true. Dreams without actions are only dreams and wishes. Dr. Martin Luther King Jr. did have a dream, but he and others also acted. Procrastination is the biggest killer of dreams. When you procrastinate, you are wasting valuable time that you can never get back. Time will not stand still and wait for you to do something. It will move on. You do not want to get left behind. So, get moving. Before you act, you must plan and prepare. Action without preparation is a disaster waiting to happen. Let's look at one way to get started:

Start Your Business

If it's a business you desire to start, create what is known as a business plan. A business plan is simply a roadmap to success for any business. It is also what you will need if you require funding from a bank or supporters. In summary, I call it:

The Five "Ws" of a Business Plan
What, Who, Where, Why, and When:

What, Who, and Where are all interrelated. They are the identification of a product and services and the people *(target market and location)* you plan to offer *(sell at the right price)* these products and services to. It is about you and your key people's *(management team)* ability to successfully operate and manage the business. For success, you and your team must be capable. Let's call it your "Dream Team." The most important thing when putting together a Dream Team is diversity. Remember, I said, *"without diversity; there is no growth. Like trees need, sunlight, air, water & soil to grow, we need each other's diverse skills, talents, experiences, and ideas we bring to the table for growth. It creates innovation".* Think about it. If no one had ever been different, we all would still be living in caves chiseling out picture messages on rocks. The world is ever changing. If everyone on your team was the same, how will you grow? At least, one person needs to be smarter than you.

What's in a name? You must choose a winning name and slogan that tells people what business you operate. For example, if you plan to offer accounting services, it should be XYZ Accounting, etc. You should register this name with the state where you plan to operate. Be aware that you cannot use a name that is already being used by another business.

Why should anyone invest in your product and service? Why is it better than the competition? It is a financial assessment and your long-range projections of returns on monies that you will invest in your business.

When is about your plans to organize and implement action steps necessary to be successful. You must set goals and make them S.M.A.R.T. *(specific, measurable, attainable, relatable, and time sensitive).*

The answers to these five questions will require a lot of research and preparation on your part. Look at it this way, anything worth having is worth working for it. If you do not know where to start with your business plan, there are explanations and templates on the World Wide Web. You can type in "how to create a business plan" in your favorite search engine. I know we have all used search engines to find out what was going on with our favorite celebrity; now you can use it for you. If you are not familiar with search engines, ask someone or visit your local library. Some templates are free, and some are not. Local communities sometimes offer free workshops and classes. Depending on the scale of your project, there are also experts and businesses that provide these services for a fee.

Now that you have planned, prepared, and obtained your start-up costs, there is nothing left to do but proceed *(act)* and persist. You must believe in your dreams. Staying positive will result in your best efforts. Remember dreams plus continued actions equals reality. Use what I like to call:

The Five "Ps" of Success
Plan, Prepare, Proceed and
Persist Positively.

The Courage to Live

FAITH gives me the courage to live life to its fullest on my terms . . .

I'm throwing caution to the wind.
Rewards will be great; it's just a matter of when.
Adventure always leads to fulfillment in the end.
It's about now not then.
Hope resides deep within.
Determination and effort will bring success
    again and again.
In enjoying this life, FAITH gives me the
    courage to seek and obtain my happiness, live
    and win.

There is not a moment to waste,
Live Your Happiness.
Have the courage to S.O.A.R.
(Seek Opportunity and Rise).

CHAPTER 5

Have Faith and Determination

I *have always believed in "stacking the deck." Faith should be at the beginning of everything you start.* Beyond my talents, some things have happened in my life that can only be explained by a divine, higher being. I am respectful of all religions and respect a person's right to worship as they please. The one thing that I do know is that there is growth in positivity. In most religions, there are positive guidelines that only enhance our lives. Faith is the key that unlocks the gate to heaven's treasures. It is also important to remember that faith without effort is useless. You put forth your best effort because you have faith it will work. However, you must combine work with the right actions.

Determination is our beliefs in our vision which leads to our persistent actions. Persistence regardless of our circumstances will lead us to success. People sometimes stop when success is ahead. You may have to readjust your plans, but you must not quit. The bottom line for success is that you must be determined to succeed no matter what the circumstances and keep moving forward.

Interpersonal Relationships are the gateway to opportunities for your ideas. Let us talk about interpersonal relationships and when they go wrong. At some point in your life, you will experience conflict in your interpersonal relationship whether it's in your business or personal life. While all humans deserve equal rights, we were not all created equal regarding talents and ideas. In life, you must first learn that you cannot change others. Therefore, it is a waste of your valuable time to attempt to do so. All you can do is convey to the other party how what they said, did or are doing makes you feel. Only they can change themselves. Beyond that, you need to keep it moving and don't let what they say about you get you down and what they do to you keep you down. The only person you can change is yourself. You must have faith, hope and be determined to succeed.

Conflict in relationships will occur sooner or later. Communication is key to the success of interpersonal relationships. Here are a few tips to help increase your communication skills during conflicts:

- **Speak kind words and be aware of your body language and actions.** No name-calling, shouting, screaming, bullying *(throwing things or intimidating)*, or intentionally bringing up known weaknesses or sensitive issues *(known as "hitting below the belt")*. No rolling of the eyes, throwing up the hand in the other person's face *(as in "talk to the hand")* or laying on of the hands *(as in hitting)*.

- **Listen.** Do not walk away while the other person is trying to communicate. Do not intentionally cut them off while they are communicating. You will need to listen actively. One way to actively listen is to restate back to them what you understood them to say. Communication is always a two-way street. Sometimes you will learn it was all a misunderstanding.

- **You should find common ground.** Usually, in most conflicts and arguments there is a common ground you will both share. This common ground is a good starting point. If it is in the workplace, does the issue violate an organizational policy or procedure?

- **Use "I" instead of "You"** when stating your feelings to avoid the other person from being very defensive or counterattacking you. When you use the word "You," it accuses and blames the other person. No one wants to feel like the bad guy even if they are. For example, say, "I understood what was said to be XYZ and that made me feel sad."

- **Focus on the present** as opposed to past grievances. Don't dwell on the past unless you are trying to show a pattern of behavior that has continued. Sometimes people's past is their present and future. They just have not gotten it yet and have no plans of modifying their behavior.
- **Avoid saving up hurts and hostilities** as future weapons and then dump them on the other person all at once.
- **Avoid pushing each other's buttons.** If you have gotten to know the person, you know what to say that will make them mad. *(Always think before you speak.).*
- **Admit when you are wrong & apologize**.
- **Don't skip around the "mulberry bush."** Say what you mean and mean what you say.

Surviving the storm is easier if you always believe *(stay positive and focused)* and keep the faith and be determined. You must believe that your situation will get better and take the necessary actions to make it so. What your mind can conceive, you can achieve. You must know that you are BETTER than any storm that has shown up in your atmosphere. My writing was my outlet during my storm. Given your capacity, you must press on despite your circumstances and remember that your journey is uniquely yours and don't compare yourself or your journey with anyone else. I offer the following poems as motivation, inspiration, encouragement, empowerment, prayers, and affirmations to help you through your storms:

<u>Determined</u>

I am . . .

Determined to believe.
Determined to achieve.
Determined to succeed.
Determined to give.
Determined to stay active.
Determined to live.
Determined to set my visions free.
Determined to be all that I can be.
Determined to be me.
. . . determined!

Be determined, and you will succeed.
Determination leads to persistence.

<u>Can't Stop Me</u>

Like a free spirit searching for an identity,
you can't stop me from my reality.
Like the clock of time that ticks on toward
eternity,
you can't stop me from my destiny.
Like the continuance of infinity,
I won't let you stop me from being all I can be.
Try to stop me, won't stop me, can't stop me!

If you allow others to stop you,
you become just like them.

Motivation

Driven by a force like a stampede
initiating behavior that's meant to succeed.
Empowering a jumpstart and taking the lead
to fill a necessary but lacking need
while achieving goals or performing a good deed.

Motivation is the driving force of action.
Action is the master key to all success.

No Escape

There is no escape from the urge to be great.
Opportunity's knock has become the shackles, and
it won't wait.
Your efforts will help to seal your fate.
Time is ticking, and you can't be late.
There is no escape, and this fact should not be a
debate.
This theme should always be your mind's state.
Success alone is a good bait.
Although naysayers will tend to hate.
There is just no escape from the urge to be great!

It's not about what you can't do;
It's always about what you can do.

Beacon of Hope

In your eyes I see all the hurt and pain;
Yet, in your eyes, I see the love and joy that remain.
In your eyes I see the struggle over the years to cope;
Yet, in your eyes, I see faith and hope.

*Eyes filled with faith and hope are eyes
that can see possibilities.*

After the Storm

After the Storm, the sun always returns to shine
without rhyme or reason,
ushering in the birth of a new season.
What has been broken and destroyed,
shall once again one day be enjoyed.
Life mimics Mother Nature's cycle of rebirth,
to start anew and replenish the earth.

After a storm, the sun always shines.

A New Day to Strive to Thrive

Every day is a great day to be alive!
I know the Sun is still shining when I open my eyes;
Rising above the horizon, ushering in the light of a
new day to strive to thrive.
Oh, the warmth of it slowly dressing up the sky.
Life, healing, & opportunity resides from basking in
its radiant rays, a feeling you can't deny.
Ah, the comfort in knowing that with each dew drop
that falls the sun shall always rise.

*A new day brings new opportunities to
strive to thrive.*

R.O.A.R.

I Am DETERMINED, See Me:
Rise above my circumstances
Own my destiny
Always spread love
Reach for the stars and beyond

Imagination

Through the window of my mind, I see a vision of
things yet to come.
Speaking to me to act in rhythm,
as though it was a drum.
Mental images of dreams not yet realized
prancing in my head!
If I do not do something, it will only lead to dread.
A conceptual utopia is hoping to be realized.
It won't stop until it has materialized.

If you can imagine it, with continued
actions, you can achieve it.

Action

Do something! Do something!
Your imagination begs of you.
It won't let you stop until your dreams come true.
Fill in the gaps! Fill in the gaps!
Your imagination pleads.
It's only trying to get you to fulfill its realization's needs.
Be proud! Be proud! Hard work was a catch.
Imagination and action are such a perfect match.

Action is the master key to all success.
It is the gap between
imagination and realization.

Circumstances

Be a product of your decisions and
rise above your circumstances.

*It doesn't matter what cards life deals you,
what matters is how you play them.*

A Hater's Prayer

Lord, thank you for all that I am and,
For giving me the wisdom not to allow my haters
to alter my self-worth.
They know not how to love.
Touch their hearts so that they too may enjoy
happiness and spread love. Amen.

Modified Serenity Prayer

Grant me the serenity to accept the fact that
I cannot change others,
The courage to change those things I can,
That I want to see in myself and
The wisdom to recognize with whom
my time is better spent,
That will make all the difference. Amen.

*Don't waste valuable time. Keep Moving.
You can only change you.*

H.O.P.E.

If YOU
Hold On, Positivity Endures
Hold On, Pain Ends

*Two messages of love from
the heart to the brain.*

Good Morning Me

Good Morning me, how was our rest last night?
We have a great day ahead of us if we don't lose sight.
Did we get up on the right or wrong side of the bed?
Are good thoughts or bad running through our head?
As I look in the mirror, here's what I see,
a beautiful person inside and out and in you, I believe.
We will empower others today, so they too can achieve,
to make our world better so that all can receive.

*When you empower others, you make the
world better around you.*

I Thank You

For every day I rise, I thank you.
For overcoming all the hatred & lies, I thank you.
For every step I take, I thank you.
For every way I make, I thank you.
For every mountain, I climb and hurdle I clear,
I thank you.
For every walk without fear, I thank you.
For every goal I reach, I thank you.
For every child I teach, I thank you.
For every soul that lifts, I thank you.
For all life's gifts, I thank you.
For every opportunity, I thank you.
For family, friends, and community, I thank you.
For strength, courage, & determination,
I thank you.
For education and dedication, I thank you.
For salvation and good decisions, I thank you.
For all that I am and my visions, I thank you.
For making life complete & whole, I thank you.
From the depths of my soul, I thank you!

*Despite circumstances, life still holds
many blessings. Always have
deep gratitude and
always be thankful.*

<u>On My Knees</u>

On my knees, I pray,
send some joy and happiness my way.
Fill the world with peace and love,
as only you can do from above.
Through my struggles and triumphs,
I have found strength.
It has helped me to go the length.
Patience is a virtue, I know, but sometimes I can't
seem to wait.
But, when all else fails, there is faith.
*With faith, through struggles and triumphs,
you can find strength.*

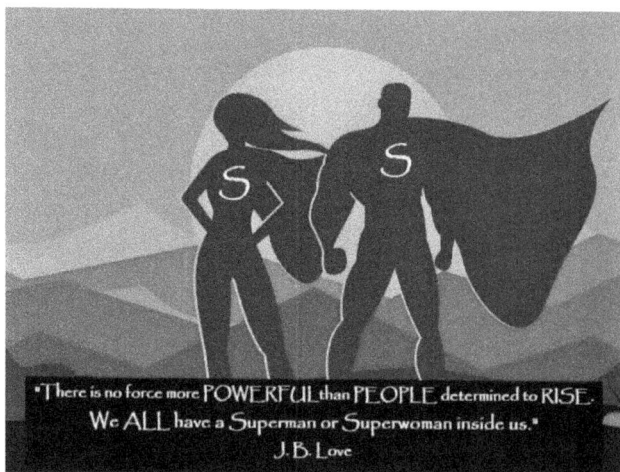

"There is no force more POWERFUL than PEOPLE determined to RISE.
We ALL have a Superman or Superwoman inside us."
J. B. Love

*Repeat after me: "I will be the powerful force that I am. I
WILL look inside my circumstances and FIND the
OPPORTUNITIES ".* **Rise and Stay Up!**

Grind to Shine
(Survival is Everything)

Every day in the world, a mogul wakes up. He/she knows they must outperform the fastest growing competition or be overtaken. Every day in the world, the competition wakes up. They know they must grind quicker than the slowest growing mogul, or they will not survive. It doesn't matter whether you are the mogul or the competition. When the sun rises, you'd better be grinding if you want to survive and shine.

Never Become Too Complacent

CHAPTER 6

Never Become Too Complacent

You see, you want; you grind, you get! It's that simple. You must keep grinding. Survival in business is about growth in an ever-changing world. People's needs change, and you and your product or service need to remain a perfect fit to meet these changes in needs. You need to stay abreast of what is going on in the world that may affect you, your products or services. You need to do the following for yourself and your team members:

- **Subscribe to trade magazines**. *Most offer online subscriptions.*
- **Attend workshops & training seminars.** *They are offered either in person or online.*
- **Visit online sites of the competition.** *You can bet they are constantly grinding.*
- **Invest in your employees.** *Pay them a competitive salary, send them to workshops, recognize & create opportunities for them.*

I've been using the concept of never becoming too complacent since I was an undergrad in college my senior year. I will never forget I had a Management Seminar class in which the class individual group grade counted for 60% of the grade. Each team had to conduct a seminar/workshop at the end of the class. I was a team leader, and when everyone else was fighting to go first, I petitioned the instructor for my group to go last. I wanted to go last because I wanted to see what the competition was presenting and how they were doing it. My team was able to adjust our mock seminar to set us apart from the rest of the field. We won the competition and received an A for the class. In fact, I graduated ranked number one in my graduating class in undergrad in college.

Sometimes when people become too comfortable at work they do the following things that can cost them their job or make them obsolete:

- Taking too many personal phone calls
- Excessive web surfing at work; especially using Twitter, Instagram, & Facebook. Never tweet, "I hate my boss," if you want to keep your job.
- Job hunting while at work
- Drinking on the job
- Always blaming others instead of accepting responsibility
- Being inflexible. Having the "Who Moved My Comfort Zone Syndrome."
- Being incompetent and undependable

which probably means they lied on their job application or resume

- Having affairs in the workplace; especially if it is against company policy
- Gossiping in the workplace; especially about their boss
- Threatening or bullying in the workplace which sometimes leads to violence. I've seen someone cussing and hitting the boss or co-workers
- Letting their appearance go
- Arriving late for work
- Being absence for work too often
- Staying on a dead-end too long
- Not keeping up with the changes in the marketplace

The same professionalism it took to get the job, the promotion, or the network connection is the same professionalism you will need to keep it unless your goal is to become obsolete or get fired.

Use Time Wisely

Avoid the Valley of the Nays

Nayseers – Will Never See Your Vision
Naydoers – Will Never Contribute
Naysayers – Will Only Offer Negativity

*Use your time and energy on things that
further your goals, not on people and things
that suck the energy, spirit, and creativity
from you.*

CHAPTER 7

Use Time Wisely

Time is a valuable commodity, so don't waste
it. Make good use of it. Simply do something.
Your success will depend on you conquering
four time-wasters: procrastination, idleness
distractions, and laziness.

Procrastination is the biggest killer of dreams. It
is the act of postponing things for a later date.
Sometimes, people never act on the deferred plan or
goal. When the delayed time comes, they defer it to a
new future date. It is impossible to succeed if you
never start. You can't count on tomorrow, so the time
to start is today.

Idleness is time spent idle waiting for other events
to occur. When people say they don't have time, they
are not taking advantage of idle time or wasting time
on distractions. Let us talk about finding the needed
time. There is no such thing as not having enough

time. You can find the extra time if you look. You can find some time when you are in the waiting room for an appointment. You can find time while you're on public transportation to and from your destination. You can find time while you are waiting for that car repair. You can find time while you are under the hair dryer at the beauty salon. You can also find it while you are on your breaks at work. If you took 10 minutes daily of your idle time and used it on your dream or big idea, that is 3,650 minutes yearly which is the equivalent of over two and half days spent on your goals. I only used ten minutes as an example for easy calculation. Take advantage of opportunities when they present themselves. Remember to carry a pad, pencil, book, or whatever you need to work on and be ready to take advantage of the opportunities.

Distractions are anything that prevents you from giving your attention to your goals. It is the circumstances that occur in your life or the people with whom you spend valuable time. Use your time and energy on things that further your goals, not on people and things that suck the energy, spirit, and creativity from you. Sometimes in life, you must march to the beat of a different drum. You can spend a lifetime trying to make someone love, appreciate or believe you to no avail. Think about it. When was the last time you spent too much time trying to be accepted, loved, and respected? Now, think about what you could have done with that time. Think BIG regarding where and with who you spend time, so you can achieve BIGGER.

If people won't let you shine in their arena, sometimes you must find another arena you can shine in or create your own.

The above is true if you know you have been striving to be the best you can be. You must learn how to handle your obstacles in the workplace, so you don't waste time getting caught up in nonsense, power struggles, or horrible circumstances. Sometimes, you need to understand when it's time to leave.

Things that happen in your life can become distractions from your goals if you allow them. Let's talk about bullying, shaming, and sexual harassment in the workplace. I have been both "skinny shamed" and "fat shamed" *(when I was sick, and my medicine cause me to gain weight)* in and outside of the workplace. As mentioned earlier, when I was younger, I was skinny. Other women would "pick at" me and call me names *(giraffe and "Olive Oyl")*. I was treated like and constantly told that I was not pretty or smart enough; regardless, it led to me becoming a model and excelling in my career. However, when I entered the workplace, it became a problem. I got my first full-time permanent job at age 21. I had completed junior college with a degree in Office Technology. I was single with no children. The women targeted me because I was thinner than them. This facility was a warehouse for a major manufacturing company, but another company employed us. I was hated, and it began to affect my career. Because they were jealous, the women would make up anything and report me to upper management. When I asked one of the women, "why do you treat me in this manner?" She replied, "You think you are something. You come in here every week with your skinny self, new clothes, expensive watches; hair always did, etc." My reply to her was "I do think I am something and so should you &, etc."

I was talented from the very beginning, and my work had caught the eye of some in upper management. They would request that I work on their projects. Before your minds stray too far, it was not about the attraction of me as a female. I was talented and dependable. They were simply attracted to my work. I started as a clerk. When I first went there, the company was keypunching serial numbers of material and its locations in the warehouse in the computer's database. I went to the supervisor and asked can the computers accommodate a scanner as it would reduce the time tremendously. Well, she felt I was being insubordinate and reported me for insubordination saying that I was unwilling to follow directions. I was warned to watch myself even though I never refused one directive given by the supervisor. It was at that point I knew this was not a facility for me for any longevity. When one of the supportive directors was out due to surgery, the others saw it as an opportunity to punish me. I was taken from an office setting and placed on the dock to drive forklifts, putting up material in the racks and loading and offloading trucks. I had never done this type of work in my life. It was done to break me and make me quit. I had a tiny frame, and in the beginning, my muscles were extremely sore. My legs would hurt badly from walking on the concrete most of the day, and I began to have severe muscles spasms. At first, I would cry in private. It was difficult for me to hop on and off the forklift and raise the tongs of the plates so that the forklift could move the plates that allowed the forklift to drive between the dock and the truck trailer. If those plates of the trailer would move out of place, it could become deadly. I complained, but they told me I should be thankful I had a job. I would hurt so badly that one day I dropped on the floor by the exit door. My body laid there almost lifeless. I could not move. The pain was horrible to bare. I had to be taken to the hospital and treated. While I was healing, I began to think differently and looked for the opportunities in this horrible situation. When I returned to work, I did not quit, yet. First, I realized that no other male had been made to work in this environment without proper training. Then, I thought about it in a "David and Goliath" kind of way. You know the slingshot and giant concept. I used something like a small lever to raise the tongs up out of a flat position by standing on it with my feet. I then started using the forklift to conduct daily audits of materials and relocate misplaced materials immediately. No one had ever done this. Instead of walking the concrete floors in the cold warehouse, I road. I cut the time required to conduct such audits in half. I also would group like materials in the same locations rather than putting locations labels on them randomly. It all made sense in my head. The processes worked so well that the manufacturing company sent someone from accounting to learn how audits were occurring at 100% now as opposed to any other time. However, the harassers began to complain that I was using the forklift to do audits and it was needed to load and offload trucks. This story was not the truth. When the plant manager that was in charge went to the foreman looking for an excuse to fire me and to ask him about my work, the foreman told him he did not want any part of this unprofessional witch hunt. He said he couldn't say anything bad about me. He told him, "heck, she can drive that forklift now better than any man on this dock. I think she is also brilliant. Since she has been doing daily audits of material, we have passed all audit by the manufacturer 100%". When the director returned, the situation was corrected. I did not have to work on the dock anymore and got a promotion to manager of a department in another part of the plant. However, now some of the men were jealous, and I began to get sexually harassed. One dock worker came to my office one day and pulled his sex organ out and told me that is what I needed and was going to get. At first, I was standing there frozen and trembling as I did not know what to do. My office was isolated from the main traffic in the warehouse. It was two bays down from any other office. If I yelled, no one could hear me. I asked him to please leave my office and let me go. He was standing exposed in the only door inside my office. He refused. He acted as if he was not worried about anyone walking in on him. I began to pray out loud hoping he had gone to church when he was little and remember what it was to be good. As he came toward and grabbed me, I kicked him in the groin. He buckled over and began to groan, and when I tried to bypass him, he went to hit me, and there was a knock on the door, and it opened. His friend had been on the other side of the warehouse door the entire time. He was the lookout, and someone was coming. The friend came in, and the worker fixed himself. The friend whose father was a bigshot in the town threatened to kill me if I reported it to anyone. "You better not tell anyone." is something I would hear throughout my life. They told me no one would believe me because it was my word against theirs. Nevertheless, I reported it anyway when they left out. It was rough. I tried to get the person who came in office's bay area who had to have seen them coming from the office say that he saw them exiting the office area, but he did not want to get involved. In his opinion, no one had physically hurt me; therefore, he chose to be a fence rider. Just as they had said, the company said it was my word against theirs. Because of the death threat, I had to get someone to pick me up from work. The plant was at the end of this long winding, isolated road. There were no security guards there. When they saw me being picked up from work, the two of them went to the front office and complained that I was having someone come to the facility to threatened them. I could not believe what was happening. How could someone who was assaulted and victimized become the accused? They told me that I could have no outside visitors at my office and all my visitors must come in at the front office which was in bay one, and my office was the last bay in the plant. The door to the outside was locked. Locking this door was a fire hazard. I had to seek legal representation. Now the supportive director was not supporting me anymore. I knew I must leave this place. However, I remained focused. I started carrying mace on a keychain and a recorder on me. I continued to have someone pick me up or trail me home. The two guys left the plant. I enrolled in a senior college to become more diversified and started to look for a better opportunity. It did not take long. Within two months when that director was retiring, I too left the company and landed a job with a major international company. I got references from people I had worked with from the major manufacturing company who were aware of my talents and not at the warehouse facility. When I turned in my resignation, they were asking "where are YOU going to work, doing what?" They acted like I was not capable of doing anything. I never told them. Here are some things you should never do:

- Don't tell anyone where you are going to work when you are leaving a job, especially a horrible one.
- Don't waste your time staying in horrible situations too long.
- Don't waste your time wallowing in self-pity. Cry if you must in private but stay positive, true, stay "uniquely you" and it will work out for your betterment.
- Don't waste your time allowing anyone to make you forget who you are or can be as a person.

- Don't waste your time worrying about what naysayers think or say, especially if you know it is not true. Just be your best self, pray for them, shake it off, and keep moving.

The point here is don't waste your time in situations trying to prove yourself or make someone like you whether it is in your personal life or professional life. You don't want to wake up years down the road stuck in the same rut trying to cope.

Some battles are not yours to fight. Karma can be a WITCH. No matter what anyone says about you, your character and work will speak for itself.

Karma can be a witch. Strangely, all the people involved in this situation would experience horrible events in their life. The bigshot's son was shot in the leg which took a long time to heal and left him with a permanent limp. The warehouse director had a heart attack, his son died, and his wife left him. The fence rider ended up having an aneurysm on his way to work. The sexual harasser would end up in one terrible situation after another.

Throughout my career, I have had many haters. It was not the last time I would experience hatred or sexual harassment in the workplace during my career but nothing ever to this degree on the sexual harassment issue. In our lifetime, some of us have had to face terrible things from childhood to adulthood. However, I never would have thought that I would ever have to deal with this type of "employee/danger" in the workplace. I never did anything to anyone other than coming into an organization and be the best I could be. After I left horrible situations, it is then I realized that "karma was a witch" and no matter what someone says about you, in the end, your character and work will always speak for itself.

In the spirit of moving on, let us talk about laziness. Laziness *(inaction)* is not being willing to use your energy for anything productive. Lazy people do not develop goals. They only exist. There are different thoughts on laziness:

- Bill Gates said he always chooses a lazy person to do a difficult job because they will find an easy way to do it.

- Dr. T. P. Chia says *people who are in the habit of enjoying the comfort of inaction often pay a high price in the end.*

Like Gates some people feel laziness is the mother of invention; however, like Chia, I am referring to inaction. Lazy people will give you excuse after excuse why you cannot do something or why they don't want to do something. Don't be lazy:

- Swap negativity for positivity
- Swap excuses for effort
- Swap laziness & dreams for persistent actions
- Swap talking for doing

What does success mean to you? Here is my idea of success:

S.O.A.R. *(Seek Opportunities and Rise)*

Use time wisely & unlock the treasure of your dreams

Choose right, **C**hange if needed & **C**ommit

Create a plan, prepare, proceed & persist positively

Evolve and become your best self to **E**levate

Sacrifice immediate gains for growth & **S**ee success

Simply live your best life on your terms for happiness

Life in Motion

Listen to the echoes of life's memories.
Hear the sweet sounds of life's melodies.
Feel the love of life's opportunities.
See the signs of life's journeys.
Taste the success of life's victories.
Redo, and live the best life to its fullest on your
    terms and fulfil your destiny.

Life is always in motions, beckoning us to hop
aboard and enjoy the ride. Make it the best ride.
Live the best life to its fullest on your terms.

CHAPTER 8

Live Your Best Life

It's All About the Balance

In all my years in the corporate world, I have never seen an executive make it to the top and stay there if their personal life was in shambles. There must be a balance between your business life and personal life.

If you have plans of being married, you must choose the right mate for you. Someone who is loving, supportive, secure, sufficient, confident and the two of you share more in common than you do that is different. I cannot tell you the number of times I have seen a co-worker's partner or spouse show up on the job site throwing clothes & etc. out the window or making a phone call to their boss. It is not a good business look. If you can't handle your home life, why should an organization trust you with their corporation? My book, "How to Find, Enjoy, & Keep Real Love *(A Common-Sense Guide to a Healthy*

Relationship)" gives some tip on finding the right mate for yourself.

> *A restful mind is a beautiful mind capable of extraordinary thoughts. Refresh your mind and unleash infinite possibilities.*

You must make time for yourself to rejuvenate. If you are married, spend time with your family. All work and no play does make Johnny or Susie a very tired, irritable and dull person. If you are married, all work and no play can make your significant other stray. During working hours, your focus should be on work; but when it is time to leave the workplace, it is best to leave the woes of the day inside your office or cubicle. Tomorrow is another day to start anew and worrying about things or taking them home with you will not make them any better. It will only drain you and your significant other of valuable, irreplaceable quality time. Workaholics usually do not have significant others. If they do, it is usually very convenient for the partner who prefers it that way so that they can have a life outside of theirs while they are at work, especially, if they do not work. So, leave the work at work and your personal life at home.

Living your best life will be on your terms. What is best for someone else may not be best for you. There must be a balance for you to have a happy life. The choice should always be yours.

There is Wealth in Health

You are what you repeat. Living a healthy life is a must if you are to be successful in life for an extended time. For good health you must have these things:

- A Balanced Diet and Plenty of Water
- A Balanced Life
- Plenty of Sleep
- Exercise
- Stress-less Life *(no such thing as stress-free)*
  - ➤ Avoid Negativity
  - ➤ Have great Time Management
  - ➤ Learn to Say No

If you do not know where to start, you should consult your doctor. Your health is an important key to your success. Here is my big idea of the things needed for the best life:

1. **Be Your Best Self and Smile**. *It reduces stress, promotes healthy thinking, helps with weight loss, and makes you more approachable.*
2. **Think Big and Achieve BIGGER**.
3. **Plan and Act on your dreams**. *The only way to turn them into reality. Start today.*
4. **Live a Healthy and Balanced Life**.
5. **Surround Yourself with Greatness**.
6. **Live Life to the Fullest on Your Terms**. *Only you can determine your success.*
7. **Spread Love, Everywhere You Go**. *It will come back to you twofold. Watch it grow.*

Win at Life

Think Your BIGGEST

Dream Your WILDEST

Work Your SMARTEST

Live Your FULLEST

Love Your HARDEST

Share Your HARVEST

Speak and Act Your KINDEST

Smile, Grind & Shine Your BRIGHTEST

Take Care of Yourself Your BEST

Stay You & Be Your GREATEST

The First Impression is the Lasting Impression.
Be your best and dress appropriately for the occasion.

CHAPTER 9

Dress for Success

Let us talk about professional image. It takes approximately five *(5)* seconds for someone to get a first impression of you. Your image is mostly made up of your appearance and body language including your tone of voice. If your appearance sends the wrong message, it is tough to regain someone's confidence in you. That's right. The first impression is usually the lasting impression. I cannot tell you the number of times I have interviewed candidates, and I can't remember one thing they had to say because I couldn't get past the annoying distracting, oversized accessories/jewelry, the neon colored hair, the inappropriate dress, and the loud smelling perfume or cologne. You must remember you are not going clubbing; you are going to the workplace to work. My thought process is that if the candidate did not think big enough of the organization to dress appropriately for the interview how can or will they be a good fit for the organization. Here are three essential things to keep in mind when it comes to workplace attire:

1. Know the industry you plan to work in and dress accordingly. What is appropriate dress for one industry *(entertainment and marketing)* may be very different for another industry.
2. Check your organization's dress code.
3. Dress for the job you want and not the job you currently have.

Well dressed women and men wear clothes that complement and coordinate. Here are a few general do's and don'ts for women and men in the workplace:

DO's for Women

- Clothes that fit the industry or occasion, your body type and are current
- Classic, simple lines
- Clothes that coordinate in color, fabric, and pattern:
  - ➢ Solid shades for your main pieces
  - ➢ Brighter and lights as accent & blouses

- ➢ Colors that complement your facial skin tone
- Natural or blended fabrics & no shiny or evening fabrics
- Small, medium, or blended prints and plaids
- Stockings should be neutral without patterns
- Socks should match your shoes or pants
- Make-up should be appropriate & complement your skin tone. Avoid loud eyeshadow and lipstick
- Well-groomed nails
- Accessories should be conservative and kept to a minimum
- A hairstyle that fit your face shape
- Eyeglass frame shapes that are flattering on you

DON'TS for Women

- Distracting or overbearing clothes or accessories (*Anything that is too revealing, too tight, or too clinging & large jewelry*)
- Wearing too much perfume
- Messy or dramatic hairstyles; especially with rainbow highlights

- Evening looks including shiny or evening fabrics

Something that was helpful for me is that I created a look book album and purchased a staging rack. I went to my closet and put together looks of every combination including shoes. I took pictures and placed them in an album. I staged my outfits for the week based on the season and weather forecast. I would move the picture sleeve to the rear at the end of the week. The goal was not to repeat the same look within two weeks. I would start again for the next week. You can also stage for vacations and business trips. I have narrow feet; therefore, when I found a low heel shoe or loafer that was perfect, I purchased it in multiple colors and quantities. Gone was the daunting task of trying to find something to wear in a closet full of clothes each morning.

DO's for Men:

- Clothes that fit the industry, your body type and are current
- Pressed shirt, suit, socks and shoes that match
- Wear pants that fit and do not sag below the waist *(i.e., put on a belt.)*
- Groom hair, hands, and nails
- Clean shaven or very groomed bearded
- Conservative Jewelry

DON'TS for Men:

- Wrinkled clothes
- Untucked shirt or shiny evening fabrics
- Wearing a dress shirt and cotton pants
- Go sockless or socks & shoes that do not coordinate with a suit
- Wear too much cologne
- Messy hair or dramatic hairstyles
- Oversized Chains, Rings, & Watches

For men and women, a mirror will be your best friend. You should get a floor length mirror and check yourself before you exit your home for the public. If you can see through your clothes, so will others. If you can see that your clothes are wrinkled, so will others. If you got dressed in dim light, and you see that you have on mixed match shoes, so will others. Also, you should keep an extra blazer, outfit, and comfortable shoes at work or in your car for emergencies.

Travel Tips for Men and Women

You must check your airline and Transportation Security Administration, TSA's, guidelines for air travel. But here are general guidelines:

Only take durable carry-on luggage. It will save time at the airport by avoiding baggage claim.

Keep a toiletry bag always packed that you never remove from the luggage. Check TSA's rules for liquid containers. If you do not want your stuff confiscated and to be held up at the security line and possibly miss your flight, you should follow TSA's 3-1-1 rule for carry-on luggage? Familiarize yourself with this rule: All liquids brought onto planes must be in 3.4-ounce bottles or smaller and inside a single, clear, quart-size zip-top bag. You will also want to check with the hotel in advance to see what toiletries and grooming items *(blow dryer, etc.)* they provide. The hotels usually have an iron, but I don't like to use hotel irons on my clothes. I use a small travel steamer. Also, if you forget your steamer, you can hang your clothes in the bathroom while you shower to help with wrinkles.

If your stay is extremely long and you must take check-in luggage, get matching durable luggage. It looks bad when a colleague picks you up at the airport, and your luggage does not match and is falling apart held together by electrical tape. Even though it might seem hard to believe, I have seen this happen.

Pack clothes you can wear with the same accessories. If your trip is short, wear one pair of casual shoes that go with everything and pack one dress shoe that goes with everything. Wear one casual blazer that will go with every casual outfit for down times. Also, for women, I would carry a tote purse/bag that my laptop could fit into along with my other necessities.

Women should create makeup palettes. I use a certain make-up brand, and they have a system where you can create palettes. I have created lipstick & eyeshadow palettes combinations with enough room in the palette to include mascara & lip pencil & etc. There is no need to have these items separate and search for them to use them. I use this same system at home. It is a great time saver.

You should always dress as though you have already made it. You can do this on a budget. You need to be smart about it and not waste your money on too many fads and trendy items. For the corporate workplace, women should always invest in what I will call wardrobers. Some men departments are still using this term in retail stores. Wardrobers are collections of clothing items usually classic/simple pieces that can be mixed and matched together *(i.e., suit jacket, skirt, pants, dress and sometimes vest)*. If they are classic, they will have longevity as they will always be in style. It gives you the biggest bang for your money. I own wardrobers in classic solid blue, black, dark grey, brown, ecru, and red. It gives me almost an endless option of mixing and matching. Invest in suits and shoes. Never skimp on these items. You can purchase these items on sale, but you should never skimp on the quality. I own a few classic, quality blazers I have had for over ten years. To date, people still compliment me on them and ask where I purchased them.

Shop on a Dime & Look Like a Million

You do not have to break the bank to dress for success. Department stores, discount stores, and online retailers are always running sales. To make the dollar stretch, I do the following:

- **Shop for winter clothes and shoes in late winter and early spring.**
- **Shop for summer colors in late summer and early fall.**
- **Compare store and online prices for the big-ticket items.** If you see an item in a store, check that same item online because you usually can find it for 30 -50% below the store price. Sometimes it is cheaper in the store.
- **Become friends with sales associates in stores.** They will alert you when they are having a big sale. They will also scan coupons for your purchases even when you left the coupon at home or didn't get it in the mail. Some major department stores have personal shoppers.
- **Save store receipts and check for a price drop.** If I do pay full price for something, I usually shop at major retail chains and do not wear it within two weeks or a month, as the price often drops 30 to 50% within two weeks or a month. I shop at stores that honor this policy. However, some mom

and pop shops will tell you that there are no refunds; however, if you pay with a credit card *(not debit card)*, all you do is call the card company and tell them you tried to return something, and the retailer would not take it back. They will issue you a refund back to your credit card.

- **Sign up for discount alert sites** to alert you when an item you want has a change in price.
- **Put items in your cart and leave them there.** Retailer monitor shopping charts and will usually offer you a coupon or discount code through e-mail.
- **Ask for student or military discounts if it applies.**
- **Subscribe to retailer's e-mail list.** They will alert you to sales. Most will offer you a discount if it is your first time subscribing.

Happy shopping! Look your best & dress the part.

While looking your best, don't forget to act the part. Ethics in your daily activities regardless of how anyone else is acting will take you far in life. It is very important to remember your tone of voice and body language when communicating. If you set the wrong tone, it does not matter how you "look the part" it will be very difficult to recover from your first impression.

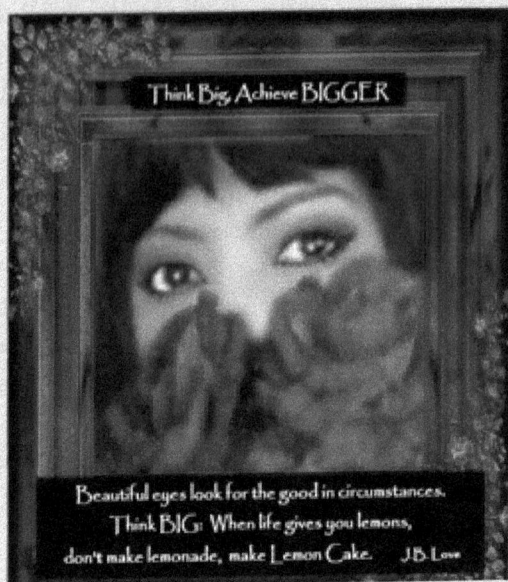

Instead of only making lemonade out of lemons, seek to make a Lemon Cake.

CHAPTER 10

What's Next

I t is time to unlock your dreams. Ultimately, what's next depends on you. Only you can define what success or greatness means to you. It is because what may mean success for you may be different for someone else. Not everyone desires to climb Mount Everest. Turning your dreams into reality has nothing to do with you being lucky or wealthy. You will find that the more you work, the luckier and wealthier you will become. As mentioned earlier, some claim that you don't need skill or intelligence to succeed; however, for longevity, it is required. It takes a current skill set, smart work, continued action and excellent networking skills. The best life is being able to live life to the fullest on your terms. Do more than exist, live!

Real success comes on your terms. It comes one thought at a time. Thoughts drive your will and rule your actions. If you make that thought positive and a big one, you will be on your way to achieving bigger than you ever imagined. Thinking big and achieving bigger is what it is all about. Tell yourself this about success daily:

Success is not an illusion; I can't achieve.
All that I need resides within me.
It's been here all along; I could not see.
Not seeing will keep me from my dream's reality,
not allowing me to be all that I can be.
I will succeed all because now I see, and I do believe.

All that you need to succeed resides with you.
You need to **see it, believe it** *&* **act on it**.

You should never rely on others' praise or acknowledgment to regard yourself positively. Some can't acknowledge talents in others that they desire for themselves but will not put forth the effort to obtain. Be your best self regardless and feel unconditionally good about your talents and who you are independent of naysayer's opinions of them and you. Although the right people will be a great resource, you have an innate ability to survive. On your journey, you will need independence, self-reliance, and resilience. It will help open doors to infinite possibilities and opportunities.

The worst feeling you can have is to rely on other's praise and acknowledgment of you and your talents and then complain when the outcome is negative.

I can't count the number of times others have told me after hearing about one of my projects that everyone has talent and stories as if my accomplishments are insignificant. For me, it has always been about how my experiences can equip someone else with the tools needed to elevate them on their journey in life. Success is not about the talents and stories of everyone. Success comes to those who dream and think big, pay attention to details, plan, prepare, act, and persist positively. It is OK to say good things about others, but when you only hear these things when you have made an accomplishment, there is something wrong with that picture. Sometimes people do not know enough about the subject matter at hand to give a good opinion, and other times they are too educated *(as in know-it-all)* to see another viewpoint. As mentioned earlier, everyone that has an education is not intelligent. You should always remember there is a difference between education and intelligence and not be so hard on yourself when others try to make you feel insignificant. It is crucial that you stay positive and never give up. Think of the following when you think about what "they say":

<u>The House of They</u>

On any street anywhere in the Valleys of the Nays,
    you can be assured to find a "Circle of Them"
    that resides in "The House of They."
It is where people are spreading their gospel as if it is
    the truth and the only way.
"They" have traded sharing love for spreading lies
    because that's all "they" know and their goal is
    always to lead you astray.
Always remember, "Who are 'they' anyway?"
Their actions are not unique and true meaning do
    "they" rarely convey.
The only real power they possess is what you give
    away.
"They" never mean you any good on any given day.
"They" can't see your vision and negativity is the only
    thing "they know how to portray.
Naysayers will become your footstools if you
    remember to ignore and keep them at bay.
Life should be about the discovery of "what is" and
    what "you" have to say.
Never let a small mind dictate as "they" do not
    contribute, and "they" are only trying to betray.
Keep your head up, have faith, determination,
    courage, and pray.
These actions will give you the power to rise, stand,
    and stay.

Make your Naysayers stepping stones to something great:
Avoid the Valley of the Nays:
Nay Seers, Naysayers, & Nay Doers

Remember that the road to success starts with a BIG idea. I hope this book has pointed you in the right direction. Unlock the treasures of your dreams and BIG Ideas. Go ahead and make the right choices to fulfill your destiny by:

- Embracing Yourself and Your Uniqueness
- Being Your Best Self
- Dreaming and Thinking BIG
- Overcoming Obstacles
- Planning, Preparing, Acting, Persisting Positively, Elevating, Succeeding & Repeating

Maslow said, *"What a man can be, he must be."* There will be no limits if you make it so. The grass is always greener where effort is applied. Your goal in life should be to maximize your potential on your terms. Elevate by using obstacles, ignoring doubters, overcoming circumstances, learning from your mistakes and working smarter. Let's go. It's the only way to grow!

Elevate

It's never too late to be great.
Why wait, settle for second-rate or be adequate.
When you can re-create, evolve, be your best self & elevate.

Can't celebrate until you elevate.

Remembering the tips from my *The ABC's of a Healthy & Happy Life* will aid you on your road to success on your terms:

The ABC's of a Healthy & Happy Life

"**A**"lways smile, act,

"**B**"e your best self, be self-reliant & balance work & personal life.

"**C**"hoose right, change if needed & commit *(growth needs)*.

"**D**"o more than exist, live and don't let

"**E**"gotism

"**F**"uel your mind & wreck your dreams & relationships.

"**G**"ive yourself permission to live life to the fullest on your terms.

"**H**"ave

"**I**"ntegrity and independence.

"**J**"ust

"**K**"eep

"**L**"iving your best life &

"**M**"aking a difference.

"**N**"ever give up or become too complacent.

"**O**"mit skipping yearly check-ups, healthy meals & exercise.

"**P**"ray, plan, prepare & persist positively.

"**Q**"uit over-committing.

"**R**"id your space of negativity & remember the difference between education & intelligence.

"**S**"pread Love, stay positive & surround yourself with greatness. *(Never be the smartest person in the room.)*

"**T**"hink BIG & Achieve BIGGER.

"**U**"se resilience, time wisely, obstacles & live with

"**V**"alor" *(great courage).*

"**W**"alk in the truth, lies are harder to dress up.

"**X**"-Ray

"**Y**"ourself & improve what you can.

"**Z**"ero in on your skills & evolve and elevate.

Think BIG Action Plan Worksheet

DREAMS + CONTINUED ACTION = REALITY
ACTION – PREPARATION = DISASTER

THINK BIG, ACHIEVE BIGGER
What are my dreams and aspirations?
(Hint: What do you want to become, what skills do you have/want or what do you have a passion for?)

USE AVAILABLE RESOURCES
How much do I know about my dream and where and how can I learn more?

USE TIME WISELY
Where am I currently wasting time & where can it be better used?

Where can I find extra time?

PLAN, PREPARE & ACT
What do I need to do to turn my dream into reality?

What am I going to do today to begin my journey?